Failing to Win

RETHINKING CHILDREN'S MINISTRY

Brenda M. Croston

Simple Truth Publishing
Nashville, Tennessee

© 2023 by Brenda M. Croston
Published by Simple Truth Publishing
A division of Simple Truth Ministries
Also operating as Croston Ministries
651 S. Mt. Juliet Rd. Ste. 198. Mt. Juliet TN 37122
simpletruthpublishing.com

Printed in the United States of America

All rights reserved. No part of this publication may be reproduced, stored in a retrieval system, or transmitted in any form or by any means—for example, electronic, photocopy, recording—without the prior written permission of the publisher. The only exception is brief quotation in printed reviews.

Library of Congress in-Publication Data

978-0-9995285-1-8
Unless otherwise indicated, Scripture quotations are from the New International Version. Copyright 1997 by Tyndale House Publishers.

Editor: Brandi Wade

Praise For Failing to Win

"Brenda's storytelling ability is excellent. This book is simultaneously personal, insightful, and deeply instructive all at a novel-like pace. This is recommended reading for Sunday school leaders and Children and Youth Ministry Leaders. In fact, I recommend this as a team building must read to help team members understand the often-unspoken dynamics that cause them to succeed or fail. *Failing to Win* [will encourage them] to take an honest look at how we sabotage others or let them sabotage themselves."-**Frank I. Williams, National African American President and Pastor of Bronx Baptist Church and Wake Eden Baptist Church, New York, New York**

"Failing to Win: Rethinking Children's Ministry, is not only a captivating read, it is a great tool for Children departments established and new. This powerful book provides a fresh look at church ministry, strategies, methods, and a philosophy that it is okay to make mistakes in order to succeed. Many times, we think that Denzel Washington or corporate America has created the mantra "if you ain't failing,

you ain't trying." However, Psalms 73:26 tells us that *My flesh and my heart may **fail**, but God is the strength of my heart and my portion forever."*-**David Cox, Sr., Pastor- Temple of Faith Baptist Church, Detroit, Michigan**

Dedicated to My SAM K. JAC

Gratitude to my God.
Father, thank you for hearing me, seeing me, and knowing me, but still using me to advance your kingdom.

Heartfelt appreciation for my husband, Mark, who always pushes me to do what God has called me to do. This project would still be on the shelf without your nudge and support.

Many thanks to Brandi Wade who labored over this book as if it were her own. Your editing clarified my words. I'm so grateful.

Friend, thank you for choosing *Failing to Win: Rethinking Children's Ministry.* Within these pages are seven considerations for children's ministry leaders and workers. This labor of love resulted from what I call, an incidental-God moment. A conversation between two mothers failing at mothering, both fully aware of the failing. Both falsely labeling the failures as final. Both unaware of the forward nudge those failings gifted us.

Foreword

Jesus said, "Suffer little children, and forbid them not, to come unto me: for of such is the kingdom of heaven (Matthew 19:14 CSB)." The life of Jesus was marked by those wanting to come close to him. Lepers. Blind men. Religious leaders. They all came. But no demographic was more special and significant in the presence of Jesus than children. He saw children not as those to be ignored because of their age, but as those to be embraced because of their hearts.

Nothing is more necessary than caring, cultivating, and covering our children. This is especially true these days as instances of molestation, parental neglect, and abuse increasingly rob their innocence. We [the church] must save the children from the aforementioned negligence and any other threatening forces.

Why?

King Solomon said it best, "Children are a heritage from the Lord." (Psalms 127:3) His words are our why. Children are not accidents. Children are not mistakes. They are a representation of God's favor.

Brenda reminds us of this truth.

When we invest in the life of our children – not just on birthdays and during Christmas – but throughout the year through the church, they will be extensions of our commitment to Christ and His church.

Children, students, and youth ministry are not for the faint of heart. However, our faith has no future without those who heed the call to this ministry.

Brenda has provided a template for those called to serve this present age and future generations.

Thank you, Brenda. -**Breonus M. Mitchell, Sr.**- **Board Chairman, National Baptist Convention, USA Inc., Senior Pastor-Mt. Gilead Missionary Baptist Church, Nashville, Tennessee**

Contents

Start Failing Here............................15
Ministry Begins with You......................21
Don't Hezekiah 35
Building Your Team 49
Trauma Circles 67
Teaching Truth 79
Ministry Possibilities-Coulds not Shoulds...91
Quit Every Day and Two Times on Sunday...103

Bonus- Besting Behaviors..................113

Start Failing Here...

Failing involves two ingredients: attempts and ineffectiveness.

It often produces one result: shame.

This had been my lived experience in my personal life and ministry until a conversation with a friend opened my eyes.

"I would love to be a fly on your wall. You guys do so many cool things together. The love you all have for one another...so sweet." -Her observation after watching a made-for-social media video featuring my family.

Leave it to social media to make a family look perfect. Except mine wasn't. Isn't.

Silence gripped the phone as these words brewed in my belly: *Girl, we are far from perfect.*

Should I tell her that?

More silence.

I contemplated how I, the pastor's wife, ministry leader, bible teacher, author, entrepreneur, could speak my truth. A truth that could drown me in misunderstanding, ruin my reputation, expose the relational dynamics of my blended family, and possibly have the culture cancel me before it ever even encounters me.

Slowly but shamelessly, I spoke the words anyway.

"Girl don't be fooled. We are —how do the kids say it—a whole mess. A loving one, but a mess all the same."

My friend's assumption that my family might be a melaninated Brady Bunch was understandable. The video highlighted a natural synergy. Our active efforts to know, love, and embrace one another shined making the video funny and endearing. She sounded surprised and relieved to hear we, like her family, dealt with not so Brady issues.

"When we truly become *The Melanin Brady Bunch: Tales of the Perfectly Blended Choco Lattes,* I'll write a book." We laughed.

Then my heart caught hold of the flippant response. I filtered it through a stream of feelings. Specifically, the "When we become, then I will…" portion—four questions emerged.

Should I wait until everything is perfect to speak about the struggles I'm having? Are the words of a testimony only effective when the test has passed? Are my family failings irrecoverably unique? Should they, or any of my failings, be kept quiet?

The answer—a bold no—brewed within. This time I did not hesitate to spew exactly what was on my mind.

"No! I'm not going to wait. Somebody needs to know they are not in the struggle alone. Whatever the struggle is." My friend agreed. "Why wait?"

"GIRL, DON'T BE FOOLED. WE ARE-HOW DO THE KIDS SAY IT-A WHOLE MESS!"

That conversation birthed *Failing to Win*. This is the first installment of a series revealing my raw and unfiltered failings. Well, maybe a little filter, but not a pretty one. Enough filter to keep you at the point of uncomfortableness without breaching the TMI zone. The point where real-life happenings happen, but many are too ashamed to admit they happen to them. That is where *Failing to Win* aims to take you with the hope that you too will discover what I learned that day.

Failing is not final. Everyone who is failing

right now needs to know that. Really know it.

My friend's relief at finding out my motherhood journey may have been more flawed than hers confirmed the need for realness. My realness. So, here it is. I am not only failing at motherhood. I am failing at ministry, marriage, entrepreneurship, teaching, and writing. All things I feel called to do. All things I feel inept doing.

Terrible, right?

Why should you read any further? Good question.

Keep reading because failing does not have to be the shameful dark space it has been painted to be. Failings, yours and mine, are repeated, refined attempts toward success. Each one produces necessary knowledge and understanding. Call me radical, but my failings have done nothing but help me. It's time I stopped mentioning them in hushed tones or not mentioning them at all. Openly admitting to failing is not terrible, but making others believe failing is not an option is.

Reality is *Failing to Win* is what I need most right now—not another testimonial from the successful wife/mother/ministry leader I aspire to be. Why? Because it's the idea of another person's "success" that fueled self-imposed expectations of perfection and almost kept me from being honest with my friend. Everyone is failing at something, but not everyone is talking about it. Forgive me [or don't] but I need reassurance that I am not the only one failing.

Don't misunderstand me to say success stories are not helpful. They are, but they are also plentiful. I have many examples—dead, alive, biblical, and secular—who are already on the other side of through, or seemingly so. I am not saying I am not grateful for the examples. I am. It's just that they are *there*, and I am *here*. I need someone here, in the trenches, alongside me. Not here with me moaning and complaining, but here with me failing and trying again. Failing to win. Since I am not seeing a lot of that, this is my attempt to be that for me and others.

Tell the truth. You're failing too. That's why you picked this book because you are trying not to fail at children's ministry and maybe even life. I can't promise a deep dive into these pages will transform you into children's ministry worker of the year with a soft propeller toward mastering life itself. That is not what this is about. Stop reading now if that is what you're looking for.

Failing to Win is an invitation to a new perspective on failing. Failing is necessary and should be embraced. Those who can't fail, won't ever accomplish anything. So, fail…to win, especially in children's ministry.

My early years of ministry were as a children's minister. I failed at it. Majorly.

I didn't tell anyone, except anyone with eyes to see, knew. Those failings yielded lessons for ministry and life. I use them as I travel the country talking to pastors, ministry leaders and workers, and Christian education directors about how to build a viable children's ministry.

I wouldn't dream of kicking this series off with any other topic; as children's ministry is my first love. I pray you will carefully examine the lessons presented here to gain a clear view of how to avoid the missteps that produced them.

Make no mistake about it, you will fail after reading this book, but not in the same ways and depths as I have, because my failures opened the doors to your wins. You're welcome. Prematurely, that is, because my fails producing your wins are predicated on what you do with the information.

I believe you will handle it with care.

Thus, I bid you adieu. May your failings be passed on so that others will win too.

Brenda

Ministry Begins with You: I failed at knowing me.

Lesson 1:

Take inventory of the stock God has given YOU.

Lesson 1:

Take inventory of the stock God has given YOU.

Ministering to children is, in my opinion, the premier ministerial task. You think God has called you to children's ministry? Consider it an honor for which you are called but approach it with humility and caution. The call does not equate to guaranteed success. God's call is an invitation to careful preparation.

Do you know who you are as a son or daughter of God? What drives you? Irks you? Scares you? What God-given traits make you you?

I Am An Eight

8

Powerful

Dominating

Self-confident

Decisive

Willful

Confrontational

That's who the Enneagram personality test says I am. Thanks to a major nudge from God, His Word, the good people at Enneagram and some other helpful tools, I'm being introduced to myself for the sake of ministry service. You should do the same.

Wait.

Maybe you have never heard of the Enneagram test. Stop reading. Type Enneagram into your search engine; read up on it. Take the test and thank me later. For the rest of you—keep reading.

I'm An Eight, Maybe

Enneagram's analysis of my personality would have served me well nearly twenty years ago when

God first called me into ministry. Had I known I'm powerful, dominating, self-confident, decisive, willful, and confrontational some of my decisions might have been different. I'm being a little facetious. Truth is there are only three of those descriptors that I can truly claim. I won't tell you which. Here's what I will tell you. I had no clue who I was, what I wanted, the extent of my capability, or what to do with who I thought I was when ministry came knocking at my door. And I did not take the time to find out before plunging into the task. I assumed God's call meant I was equipped enough.

Was I equipped? Yes, in the sense that I had God's permission to do the work. Did I know how to pair that equipping with my bends and proclivities? No. I didn't understand how my calling and being should and could work together. Nor did I realize that the call meant I had the responsibility of honing the skill God assigned to my hands. Don't make the same mistake.

First and foremost, seek to know God. It is hard to discern His direction without seeking to know Him first. Taking the Enneagram test or any other personality test won't magically change you. What it will do is provide an opportunity to self-reflect and seek God for the answers to the questions it asks.

Knowing who God is shines light on who and what He has called you to be and do. Knowing Him empowers you to ask yourself hard questions. Knowing Him equips you to answer the hard questions truthfully.

Called To Children's Ministry

Ask yourself the right questions:

1. What are my strengths and weaknesses?
2. Do I have the time to give?
3. What spiritual gifts do I possess that will move the children's ministry forward?

What Are My Strengths And Weaknesses

Approach this question from various angles.

Physical

- Do I have the energy it takes to teach a vibrant lesson?
- Can I simultaneously teach and manage behaviors?
- Am I able to set up and break down staging if necessary?
- Am I willing and able to complete ministry tasks outside of the church setting?
- Am I mobile enough to attend field trips/ministry outings?

Mental
- Am I patient?
- Am I teachable?
- Do I have a genuine desire to freely open my heart to children?
- What heart wounds/traumas are present in my life today? How might they affect how I embrace/view ministry workers and children?
- Are there any past traumas like emotional abuse or neglect that may affect how I execute and live out my role as a children's minister/leader/worker?

Spiritual
- Have I accepted Jesus as Savior?
- Do I allow the Savior to guide my life?
- Am I practicing spiritual disciplines daily?
- Do I support the mission of this church with my time, talents, and tithe?
- Do I practice the principle of Sabbath?

Do I Have The Time To Give

This question may not appear as crucial as the first. It is and cannot be trusted to a quick, thoughtless answer.

Time Analysis
- Outline your schedule starting with the sound of your alarm and ending with the time you settle down to sleep.
- Outline each day separately as each day does not bring the same activities and events.
- Check the church calendar. Note all the children's ministry monthly activities.
- Compare your daily schedule with the children's activities. Note activities that your schedule will allow you to participate in.
- Study both your personal calendar and the children's activities you deemed doable. Add the activities to your personal calendar. Estimate preparation time, including study, drive time to and from the activity, etc.

  Then ask and answer this question: Do I have the time to give?

What Spiritual Gifts Do I Possess That Will Strengthen And Advance The Ministry

I know what you are thinking. Isn't this the same as question one? No. That question required an examination of strengths and weaknesses. This question calls for specificity concerning how your gifts could enhance the ministry.

How do I know what spiritual gifts I possess?
- What drives you? Your passions are usually tied to your area(s) of gifting.
- Take a spiritual gifts test. The accuracy of the result depends on your level of honesty and self-knowledge.
- Take a personality test such as the earlier suggested Enneagram. This too requires honesty and knowledge of self, or the results will be skewed.
- Where do you see God working in your life? It is an indicator for where you should direct your gifts.
- Don't forget to pray throughout the process. God is eagerly waiting to share the correct answers.

What are the downsides to my spiritual gifts?
- Every spiritual gift is a good gift from God. However, an unhealthy mental state distorts His perfectly perfect gifts.
- Spiritual gifts are not magically muted when mental and emotional states are out of alignment.
- Acknowledge and examine any mental and emotional weaknesses.

- Be honest with yourself.
- Be honest with your team members.

If you are like me, you didn't know spiritual gifts have a downside. You need an example. One day my husband and I were discussing some family issues. He said, "You lean toward the downside of your prophetic gifting." I, being the good Christian that I am, said—and by said, I mean—yelled, "What are you talking about?"

"Those with the gift of prophecy are truth tellers and sometimes those truths are delivered rather brashly."

I didn't believe him. A few weeks later, he emailed me a complete spiritual gifts test inclusive of a chart outlining the full nature of spiritual gifts. He was right. I was flabbergasted.

Don't make the same mistake. Be aware.

Carefully review each question and the corresponding bullets. Use them introspectively.
Find out what your spiritual giftings are and all they include. Please don't rush through the process. Sit with the answers for a while.

Are you ready to take on the role of children's minister/ministry leader? Answering no does not exempt you from God's call to the task. No means you have work to do. Unhealthy leaders operating in their area of spiritual gifting can cause severe spiritual and emotional damage. We commonly refer to this as church hurt. It has caused too many young adults to equate God with harmful practices He never intended His giftings to be known for. I didn't do the necessary pre-work before accepting a children's minister position. Foolishness ensued. Here's a snippet of my story:

> Every spiritual gift is a good gift from God. However, an unhealthy mental state distorts His perfectly perfect gifts. Spiritual gifts are not magically muted when mental and emotional states are out of alignment.

God graced me with the gift of leadership. Unfortunately, He did not give me administration, its complementary gift. Managing the big picture details of children's ministry got fuzzy real fast. Even worse, before taking on the children's minister role, my gift laid semi-dormant under years of layered insecurity. Translation: my skills were as untested as a crawling toddler's walking ability— undeveloped skill, no stability. The combination of my perceived skill and the truth of my actual ability landed me in a whole lot of trouble with the children's ministry team.

The team sensed my leadership abilities which led to high-performance expectations. Once my administration skills, or lack thereof, were revealed, the high expectation was not lowered. Instead, the bar kept getting higher and higher. It was like an adult game of Keep Away. Administratively speaking, I was a toddler. The expectation bar sailed far above my stunted reach.

A year or so in, I had the bright idea to implement a popular Bible club program to replace the church's Wednesday night children and youth Bible studies. The team members were excited to get started but made the mistake of leaving most of the details to me. Why? I was the leader. They assumed I knew what I was doing because it was my idea. My insecurity prevented me from asking for help.

I should mention most of the team had what I lacked—an administrative gift.

There is not enough space to share all the ways this venture went hilariously awry. Summary-I made a lot of mistakes which frustrated the team.

It was bad. I had to laugh to keep from crying. The team didn't get the joke.

Don't tell them I said it, but it was just as much their fault as it was mine. Once my struggle was evident, no one volunteered to help. Wait. Let me clarify. Every team member showed up each Wednesday and did their assigned jobs well. The problem was no one rolled up their sleeves to help me with the miniscule details that quickly turn into huge details when left unattended. The everyday operation of developing and maintaining a viable ministry fell flat.

Let me pause the story line for a moment. Lean in close. Mentally review the three questions posed at the chapter's opening. The next portion of the story is the reason for most of the questions and examinations.

Both ministry leaders and workers need to know what everyone brings to the team as well as being aware of others points of need or weakness. Everyone should understand that their gifts are to be used to support areas of lack. Why? Because there will be someone like me—the me I was during that time—on your team. You must not do what our team did.

The team had the skill to help me but refused to do so. This wasn't a pre-calculated desire or ill intended but a manifestation of their own unresolved pain and insecurities. The Enneagram 8—dominating, powerful, willful me lured their hidden self-doubt to the surface. Additionally, my refusal to ask for help led them to believe I didn't want help. So, they let me fail.

Why? They had not taken the time to examine themselves before becoming children's ministry leaders/workers for the purpose of knowing where and when their strengths were needed for support of the overall team. What's worse is their leader [me] had not created an environment conducive to sharing strengths and weaknesses. Our team did not know one another. Our personal pain points, needs, and fears were a mystery. We only knew what we could see of one another. That led to mistrust. Everyone worked hard in their areas, but we did not trust one another enough to work together. Ultimately that was my responsibility, but I was too immature to see the real problem and fix it.

What I now know about the underlying reasons for both the team's actions and mine, I didn't know then. As you can imagine, I wasn't forgiving, and neither were they. We internalized the hurt. Hurt that I could have stopped or avoided altogether.

There were secret meetings and discussions about my failings and shortcomings. The team decided to stage a coup d'état. The church had a protocol for removing leaders involving the church board. I had not violated any moral or spiritual code, so they didn't have the evidence needed to oust me. Though not ousted, I was iced. Support for the ministry grew cold. A few of the annual children's events fell flat due to lack of volunteers and participation. Only 15 kids showed up to one of our most anticipated events of the year, rather than the usual 100-150. It was a horrible time. Planning meetings were a nightmare, each one was like walking down The Via Dolorosa (the road to the cross) for a monthly crucifixion.

All of this could have been prevented had I known who I was, my ministry capacity and deficits, and what spiritual giftings I had to offer. Had I known the right questions and examinations to ask of myself and the team, who knows what we could have accomplished.

One more thing, a cautionary note to any ministry leader:

The team possessed amazing talents and the spiritual giftings necessary to minister to children. Under my leadership, those gifts were stifled.

Ministry leader, if for any reason you thought the listed self-examinations and questionings were unnecessary, I hope that quick peek into my story changed your mind. You set the tone for the ministry. The tone you set determines how well the children will be served.

DON'T HEZEKIAH: I failed at planning.

Lesson 2:

Plan for tomorrow.

Lesson 2:

Plan for tomorrow.

Who doesn't know King Hezekiah's story (2 Kings 20:1-11)?
God sent the prophet Isaiah with the warning to get his affairs in order—death was imminent. Hezekiah reminded God of his faithful service. God relented and added 15 years to Hezekiah's life.

Familiar?

Hezekiah's story doesn't end there. It picks up in verse twelve after Hezekiah's healing. That's where our cautionary tale begins. A Babylonian Prince sent envoys to Hezekiah with letters and a gift. Hezekiah invited the visitors into the palace and

showed them all that was in his storehouses—the silver, the gold, the spices, and the fine olive oil—his armory and everything found among his treasures. There was nothing in all his kingdom that Hezekiah did not show them (2 Kings 20:13).

The envoys left and Isaiah arrived. He asked, "What did those men say, and where did they come from?" Hezekiah explained—prompting another question from the prophet, "What did they see in your palace?" "Everything," Hezekiah responded (2 Kings 20:14-15).

Hear the word of the Lord: The time will surely come when everything in your palace, and all that your predecessors have stored up until this day, will be carried off to Babylon. Nothing will be left, says the Lord. And some of your descendants, your own flesh and blood who will be born to you, will be taken away, and they will become eunuchs in the palace of the king of Babylon. (2 Kings 20:16-18).

Hezekiah responded, *The word of the Lord you have spoken is good.* But he thought to himself, *Will there not be peace and security in my lifetime?* (2 Kings 20:19)

Take a moment and think about that.

Hezekiah felt relieved because the prophet's words did not apply to him. He gave no thought to the generations to come even though his action caused the impending doom. He made no effort to plead for their lives like he did for his own.

Don't Hezekiah.

Don't plead for your life and future, then refuse to do the same for the coming generations. Think about the children and families in your church and community. Think about where the culture of this world wants to take them. Think about how much of their current plight is a result of the previous generation's actions. The church, children's ministers, and team members all have a responsibility to plead for their lives too by planning for tomorrow.

Plan the Plan

Hezekiah readily showed off material things. Like him, but unknown to me, I wanted a showy ministry. One that offered every new gadget a parent and child could want. Our church was set to build a multi-million-dollar facility. As the children's minister I was asked to join one of the building sub-committees. Our chairman asked, "If money were no object, what would you include in the children's wing?" I didn't hesitate to voice the tangible things that would make our ministry the best in the city. Just thinking about all the possibilities sent mile-wide goose bumps rippling up and down my arms. You can't see me, but I am laughing at my folly. Hindsight is not 20/20; it's 20/13…sharper than normal. I am laughing because what the children's wing needed the most it already had: gifted, God and children-loving individuals eager to share God's word. I just couldn't see it.

The Who Not The What

The foundation and sustainability of children's ministry does not lie in material possessions that rust and fade. The word of God lasts. Plan with that truth at the forefront of your mind, then start with the who, not the what.

Ask: Who is our target demographic?

The basic answer is easy. Children's ministry begins from birth through eleven years of age.

Ask: How should these age groups be divided?
Younger Preschoolers- Birth to age 2
Middle Preschoolers- ages 3 to 4
Older Preschoolers through Kindergarten- ages 5 to 6
Kids- 1st to 2nd grades
Kids- 3rd to 4th grades
Children- 5th to 6th grades

Ask: Which curriculum will best suit our needs? The basic answer. Use a curriculum with solid theology, a consideration for cognitive development, and age-appropriate activities. Chapter five has more on that. For now, you only need to know that curriculum should be in place before any classes are held.

Ask: Where will the children's ministry be housed? This is a touchy subject. Most churches do not have extra space lying around waiting to be utilized. In just about every church I have attended, a little creativity and ingenuity were employed to answer this question. I am not in your context; therefore, I can't give a definitive answer. I can, however, tell you where it shouldn't be held.

Children's bible class, activities, and the like should not be held in:

- Cluttered environments
- Dirty spaces
- Rooms without a glass windowpane in the door
- Open-access areas
- Places with busy wall designs/décor.

No Clutter Please

Cluttered spaces are accidents waiting to happen. In smaller ministry spaces, rooms have multiple uses, storage being one of them. Understood. The average church has little to no designated classroom space, much less room for storage. This is where ingenuity and creativity come into play.

Research storage options. Think about how the items within your space are used, including how often, and what kind of storage set-up would minimize the time spent arranging and/or rearranging those items. Whatever the upfront cost, it is worth the investment to prevent accidents. Pay big now or pay big later. The upfront cost will only cost money. The later cost will cost money, members, trust, or much worse, a life…something no ministry can afford to lose.

Go After The Hidden Dirt

Do I really need to say why ministry shouldn't be held in a dirty space? Yes. This mention is not intended to belittle or demean anyone. Honestly. Ministry is hard and one of the things often overlooked is the need for thorough cleaning. I can say with certainty most ministries are sprucing up on a regular basis. I am certain of it. However, sprucing and cleaning are two different things. Sprucing does not work when it comes to the areas where babies and children are being ministered to. This has always been my stance, but 2020's Coronavirus pandemonium has me dead set on it.

Your ministry needs a dedicated cleanup crew. Not the church's janitor or cleaning service. Leave the sprucing to them. After each use of the facility/room/space, toys should be wiped, floors swept/vacuumed and mopped, door handles sanitized, corners and surfaces dusted, and the space returned to order. If we were together, I would look you in the eyes and speak slowly…YOUR CLEANING CREW IS AMONG THE MOST VALUABLE OF ALL TEAMS. They make the environment safe. I am not with you. That is why I am yelling in all caps! OPERATING IN A SPRUCED ENVIRONMENT, ONE THAT LOOKS CLEAN, BUT HAS UNSEEN VIRUSES AND DUST PARTICLES WILL COST THE MINISTRY MORE THAN IT CAN AFFORD TO PAY.

Let Them Look Inside

Now that we have settled that. Why did I include a glass windowpane in that list? Again, safety. Children should not be in a room with closed doors without a way for activities to be observed from the other side of the door. If your church is unable to invest in windowpanes. Do not close the doors.

Along the same vein, open-access ministry spaces should be avoided. Two reasons: kids can easily walk away if there are too many access points, and kids can easily be taken. What does an open-access room look like? Wide open spaces with several entry and exit points. Now, it is wise to have two accessible entry and exit points, like a door and a window in case an emergency occurs that won't allow use of the door. However, rooms that have several entry and exit points without proper supervision of those points leaves the children and its workers vulnerable. If you are forced to use these types of spaces, be sure to position a team member near entries and exits.

Dump Dizzying Décor

This last one might sound odd. Beware of the décor used in children's ministry spaces. I have visited spaces with bible story depictions from the
great flood to the birth of Jesus all in the same space. Confusing.
Think of your wall space as prime teaching space. Utilize it to help convey the messages you present each week. Utilize it to display upcoming events. Utilize it to display games. But please…for goodness' sake don't make it a shrine to every Bible story that has ever been told.

Here's another thing to think about concerning the outfitting of ministry space walls. Some children and adults have attention, vision, and other medical disorders that are affected by certain patterns. I see this happening in some public-school classrooms. Teachers display striped black and white patterned borders accompanied by bright lettering. It looks great but becomes a distraction for the child struggling with attention deficit and a visual detriment to migraine sufferers.

When deciding on wall space, think soothing colors like deep blue, sky blue, muted teal, blush or pale yellow. Think "less is more" when it comes to pictures. Most importantly, know that wall space is an effective teaching tool. When used the right way, it aids learning, equipping, and encouraging.

Think of your wall space as
prime teaching space.

More Questions

Ask: What does a day in the children's ministry space look like?

Plan a routine inclusive of the time children enter until the time they leave. Begin at the end and work your way backward. Understand that this is an initial outline. Include this plan in your ministry proposal packet as a possibility. Once the ministry
team is in place, present this outline and allow the

team to have input. I can't stress this enough. Potential team members want to know you have a plan. A plan helps them to see your passion and commitment. Yet, they also want to know that plan isn't etched in stone.

Team members will want to give their input. And that is best. God created us to work in community. Your mind alone cannot adequately craft a plan that will cover every detail. I guarantee your plan is great and incomplete. Trust me. It can be both. Teams who pray, plan, and perfect plans together produce good fruit together.

Ask: How will we advertise the children's ministry?

The first advertisement should be for ministry volunteers. Use every medium available: social media, church newsletter, pastoral announcements, email, whatever message delivering devices your church uses. We will talk more about this in the next chapter, but I will say this; Don't expect volunteers to come knocking at your door just because you advertised.

Then why advertise?

Advertising gives evidence of your willingness to work with the membership. Members tend to get angry if they feel like a ministry leader is not inclusive. Even if they don't want to join your ministry, they want to know they could if they wanted to.

Sounds crazy, I know. Believe me, it's true. There's a great story behind this recommendation from my time as the women's ministry leader. I would share it, but we have to stay focused.

Run advertisements for two-three months prior to initial enrollment. Once the ministry is established, set a yearly open enrollment date. Preferably running concurrent with all other church ministries. Like a ministry fair.

Ask: What roles will the children's ministry need?

The answer depends on your ministry mission and goals and will change along with those things. Here are a few critical roles.

- Ministry leader- oversees and executes ministry mission and goals, recruits volunteers, organizes and oversees volunteer training, community collaboration, and liaison between leadership-senior pastor/youth pastor/church administrator and ministry volunteers.
- Ministry coordinator- plans outreach efforts.
- Bible teachers- self-explanatory but should include activity and class schedule planning.
- Cleanup crew- separate from church's janitorial staff. Cleans ministry areas before and after each use depending on whether the

space is a multi-functional one.

Ask: What initial training is required before team members assume their roles?

- How to Study the Bible
- How to Use Curriculum
- Safety First- securing the preschool/children's ministry environment
- CPR
- Effective Teaching

Ask: What ongoing training is required?

- Creating Fun Age-appropriate Activities
- Trauma
- Making the Most of a Multi-use Space
- Classroom Management
- Creative Zoom Meetings
- Parent Volunteers-How to Enlist Their Help in and Outside of the Classroom
- Ministry Collaboration
- Station Teaching

A Word About Vision

The prophet Isaiah told Hezekiah what the future held. God allowed him to see it and inform Isaiah from it. As a ministry leader that is your job. Look around your ministry context, observe the

happenings and seek God. Ask Him to show you the future. Don't get scared. I am not talking about you falling into a deep trance launched into a terrifying outer body experience—unless that is God's plan. I mean you should ask God to lend you divine foresight to see where the children and the families in your church are heading if things were to remain just as they are today. Take what He shows you and work backwards. Plan a ministry that will counteract lostness, family division, hopelessness,
and devastation. Then train your ministry volunteers from that vision…from that passion.

    Plan the plan.

BUILD YOUR TEAM: I failed to team.

Lesson 3:

If you build it, they *might* come.

Lesson 3:

If you build it, they *might* come.

Two of the hardest things to do are recruiting and retaining good ministry volunteers. Keyword, good. Probably because members do not believe they have the time or ability to work in ministry. That's just a guess, but a firm one. I really believe this combination sends church members fleeing from volunteering in any capacity.

The time obstacle is twofold. One, everyone is busy. Two, because busyness occupies their time, there's a fear of being roped into a ministry position without any relief in sight.

The ability obstacle is layered as well. It's not that church members don't have the talent or capacity to do ministry. It's most likely that they don't know they have it. I think the ministry label makes some people feel like they are not holy enough or spiritual enough to join a ministry team. Folks don't seem to know that whatever makes them a good employee translates to being a good ministry team member or leader. Thus, the many skills utilized in the workforce mysteriously disappear when approached about joining a ministry team.

My suppositions may not be true in your environment. Consider your context. What obstacles might the membership face pertaining to working in ministry? Pray. Ask God to reveal the obstacles and the corresponding solutions befitting your context.

Fortunately, getting children's ministry volunteers came easy for me. Thank God because nothing else presented that way. The members enthusiastically embraced children's ministry opportunities. I just wish I had known how to better recruit and manage the team. Ministry life would have been easier and more effective for them and me. Don't understand me to say ministry building and execution should be easy. It won't be. It shouldn't be. There are, however, ways to make it manageable.

Build Relationally

Jana Magruder, author of *Kids Ministry that Nourishes,* suggests looking around the congregation for couples who faithfully attend Bible study. Invite them to lunch, dinner, or coffee. Share why children's ministry fuels and drives you. Talk about the wonderful children who benefit. Passionately share the vision God has laid on your heart. Then ask. Ask them to join you in making disciples of Christ.

Build Numerically

Numbers matter when recruiting. The expected number of children. The current number of volunteers. The anticipated number of service hours. It is the matter of numbers that propels potential recruits to bow out.

"You are asking me to serve on this ministry with fifty children, only five volunteers, and without knowing how long I'll be needed, or if I will ever get a break to vacation, sit in service, or refuel.

No thanks." Says the potential recruit to the desperate, disheveled, detail-lacking ministry recruiter.

Be proactive. Once the relational invite is on the table, put a time limit on their service. A service time limit will help potential volunteers fend off burnout, anticipated, imagined, or realized, and help eradicate the fear of being stuck in a position too long. Even better. A service time limit ensures an opportunity to refuel. This is vitally important. Team members who constantly pour energy, effort, and efficiency into ministry are soon empty.

Empty vessels have nothing to give. It is mathematically impossible. Zero plus zero equals zero. It is spiritually impossible. Leaders leading on zero don't authentically praise, worship, or teach; they perform. That is wholly dangerous. Remember, 90% of teaching God's word is living it. Team members who know their time of service has an end date…know that they will have an opportunity to refresh and will feel supported as a result.

> **Team members who constantly pour energy, effort, and efficiency into ministry are soon empty.**

These individuals are more likely to give 100 percent because they have 100 percent to give. Those who don't, won't.

So…say something like, "Will you join our children's ministry as a teaching team (or whatever position) for two years? You will have at least three months off during the year, and up to three additional months that will allow you to attend an adult Bible study or worship service."

Don't let them answer yet, continue with,

"If your answer is yes, we want you to help us build the team. Starting today. Ask God to reveal couples within the congregation who might fit this role. Two months into your service time, invite them to dinner, just like we are doing here. Share your children's ministry "why" and ask them to join. Spend two months training and acclimating the recruits to the setting. Finally, ask your recruits to follow the relational recruiting model too."

This spiel, or something similar, will kill many birds with one stone:
- Shows the potential recruit that you have a plan
- Gives the potential recruit the opportunity to share in building the ministry
- Opens the door to leadership development
- Guarantees a time of rest.

To name a few.

Not everyone will say yes. Some will because of the personal invitation. Others will because they sense God's calling through your invitation. Still others will because of your passion. Do not underestimate the power of a personal invite. When done with intentionality, its numerical yields are phenomenal.

Build Strategically

The numerical build lays the foundation for a strategy I like to call, Operation Covered. It was sparked by Jana Magruder's idea. Her genius brought my flight attending days to mind and the employee scheduling system.

I am not sure how employee flight scheduling is done nowadays. Twenty years ago, schedules inclusive of the total number of flight hours, days off, cities, and exact reporting times were published monthly. Each labeled by number. They were called Lines. Flight crew members bid on three Lines listing them in order of preference. Among the schedules were Lines that did not contain trip details called Reserve Lines. Newbie pilots and flight attendants typically were awarded one of these. Unless some unlucky senior flight crew member failed to submit their bid in time, thus granting a newbie the thrill of getting assigned a Numbered Line.

Reserve Lines do not have exact trip details because Reserve is an on-call status. A Reserve flight crew member must reside within two hours of the airport in case another member gives advance notice of absence. Then there is the Ready Reserve status. This requires being at the airport standing ready to assume a crew member's position if he or she gets sick while in-flight or is a no-show for an assignment. It is these Reserve Lines that influenced Operation Covered.

A full-scale Operation Covered is achieved by following Jana's advice along with the airline's reserve scheduling method:

A ministry leader builds a team relationally. For example, Leo and Robin, ministry coordinators, invite Derwin and Lorvetta to join the team. They agree, and two months later, after much prayer, God lays Morris and Mary on their hearts. That team recruits their replacements in kind, and the cycle continues until the team is large enough to create a rotating schedule.

What does that look like for the entire ministry? Reference the sample chart.

Age Group	Ministry Coordinators	Bible Teachers	Clean up Crew
Pre-school 3-4	Leo and Robin Derwin and Lorvetta Morris and Mary	Kenneth and Belva Fred and Connie Joseph and Bianca	Clarence and Tonya Milton and Shirley Mark and Brenda
Kindergarten+ 5-6	Vernon and Cheryl Micheal and Tiffany Leroy and Shauna	James and Tiffany Michael and Beverly Horacio and Gail	Leroy and Carolyn Fred and Liz Marco and Morgan
Children Grades 3-4	Eric and Monique Dean and Beth Jerrick and Jackie	Harry and Christina Adron and Veronica Paul and Lorraine	Jerome and Kim Gary and Chequita Charles and Jackie
Pre-teen Grades 5-6	Nathan and Joanne AJ and Briana Patrick and Archalena	Cordell and Barbara Michael and Tammy Nathaniel and Isabella	Josh and Kristine Herman and Peggy Ernest and Renee

After one year of strategic building, with just the critical team members listed in the last chapter, each team member recruits four teams or eight recruits. That equals thirty members. Those thirty continue building relationally and strategically. Considering retention rate averages, after two years, the team might have sixty-four active members divided into smaller teams of six and assigned a name, color, or a symbol to signify which team is which. Every team would teach/serve for two months, stand Ready reserve for one month, and Reserve for one month.

- Serving Team: Lead team- carries out duties in their designated areas of service, i.e. teaching, coordinating, or cleaning.
- Ready Reserve: Assists serving team- present in the classroom/serving area stands ready to step into the serving position in case of absence or sudden illness.
- Reserve Team: On call- able to attend worship service but steps in if a ready reserve member moves into a serving team slot or is unable to attend all together.

Sample Ready Reserve Schedule
Pre-School Team

Service Month	Serving Team	Ready Reserve Team	Reserve Team
January	Blue **Ministry Coordinators:** Robin and Leo **Bible Teachers:** Ken and Belva **Clean up crew:** Clarence and Tonya	Orange **Ministry Coordinators:** Derwin and Lorvetta **Bible Teachers:** Fred and Connie **Clean up crew:** Milton and Shirley	Sapphire **Ministry Coordinators:** Morris and Mary **Bible Teachers:** Joseph and Bianca **Clean up crew:** Mark and Brenda
February	Blue	Sapphire	Orange
March	Sapphire	Blue	Orange
April	Sapphire	Orange	Blue

Get the idea? Amend the reserve schedule according to the number of team members. No need to wait until the team is "large". Begin implementing the rotation when you have enough team members to accommodate it. However, a written schedule should be in place even at the beginning stages when teams tend to be smaller. The same is true for the service time limits. Adjust those accordingly too. The charts are an example of what the building and ready reserve schedule could be.

At some point, the original team members should merge to form the leadership team. They are no longer recruiters but still have the responsibility of growing and expanding the ministry. Their duty is to help the children's minister/pastor/director grow the vision.

Two fun facts before we move on.

One- the chart contains names of real-life married couples who I either know, love, and respect or just simply respect from afar. Two-the husband-and-wife cleanup crews are mighty men and women of valor. I put their names there to reinforce the crew's importance to the children's ministry. The job can't be trusted to just anyone.

Build Exponentially

"How can we expand our ministry team?" used to be a frequently asked question. It has now morphed into, "How can we expand our ministry team post COVID?" Feels strange. Who would have ever thought phrases like social distance, mask mandates, or quarantine time would settle in our everyday conversation and affect how we do every part of life?

Who knows what will fill COVID's spot twenty years from now?

"How can we expand our ministry team post [insert next major thing here]?"

Whatever the question filler may be, my answer has not changed. Pre-COVID, post COVID, post whatever the next life interrupter—expand your ministry inside and outside of the church walls.

That's it.

That's my answer for all eternity...through major catastrophes...and in times of peace. Expand your ministry by looking inside and outside your church. Who is seated near and adjacent to the ministry with knowledge that will empower the mission? Grab those folks and invite them in.

I wish I could take credit for this idea. I can't. This is not new; it's networking. But like our capacity to transfer our secular work into ministry, we forget how to network the moment a ministry label is attached.

What do I mean? The most effective ministry has tentacles that reach out into the congregation and community to recruit quasi members. Members who are not working in the ready reserve rotation but can offer valuable insight and inroads.

Want to expand your team? Look around your congregation for public school teachers, occupational therapists, pediatric nurses and doctors, and therapists who do not want to commit to working with children directly but will agree to train the team on subjects pertinent to children and the ministry you offer.

Want to expand your team? Look around your community. Connect with the neighborhood mama, local school principal, school social worker, college campus minister/ministry. These individuals have insight into the children and families who have needs.

Why are these eight individuals the perfect non-member ministry members? The better question to ask and answer is what can they do for the ministry?

- Public school teacher- train team members on composing lesson plans, classroom management, teaching techniques, and behavior management.
- Occupational therapist- train team members in creating age-appropriate activities to strengthen fine and gross motor skills.
- Pediatric nurses and doctors- help establish medical emergency procedures and policies. to ensure students and ministry workers are cared for well during medical emergencies and provide CPR training.

- Therapists- offer training on identifying emotional triggers and the best language to use in various stressful situations.
- Neighborhood mama/daddy- they have connection, relationship, and established trust within their community. He/She will give the ministry workers access to neighborhoods and individuals otherwise unreachable.
- School principal- a conduit to neighborhood parents and school board officials. Gives access to the student population.
- School social worker- another conduit to neighborhood parents as well as an inroad to establishing various types of truancy ministries. Also, this individual could offer training on behavior management.
- College campus minister or College gospel choir leader- He/she could direct college students to your ministry to act as aids, teachers, cleanup crew, etc.

Bottom line: the work of the ministry requires various skill sets and connections. Doing that work well mandates us to carefully observe our surroundings, taking note of areas of deficit and strength then plugging in the right individual(s) to strengthen and enhance said work.

Build Visionally

Is visionally a word? Probably not, but it works for my intent and purpose. Go back to the final thoughts under build strategically. The original team members turned recruiters turned leadership team are vital vision builders.

How? They have moved from the trenches of children's ministry and now have an aerial view.
The leadership team looks at the whole picture to discover what is working, what's not. They also have insight into the team members' gifts and abilities.
This vital information should be used to see where God wants the ministry to go.

For example, the lead ministry coordinator sees that one of his team members is fluent in American Sign Language (ASL). That information is brought back to the leadership team only to find there's a deaf child who does not attend any of the children's ministry activities because of the communication gap. The team prays about whether to train more team members in ASL to open the ministry to the hearing impaired.

Another example. The lead cleanup crew member discovers that one of the team members makes natural cleaning products. That information is brought back to the leadership team only to find that there had been some discussion about the potential harm some of the harsh cleaning chemicals might have on the children. The team prays about whether they will switch to the team member's natural products which will help said team member launch a business. Grateful, natural-soap-making team member may sponsor class materials or another need within the children's ministry. Just to say thank you.

These examples are hypothetical but possible. The point is team leaders have an opportunity and responsibility to diligently seek God to grow deeper fellowships and expand the ministry services being offered. This helps the children's minister/director/pastor/ to see needs that otherwise would be missed because it is impossible to be in every place at once. A team of leaders' eyes are sharper, wider, and clearer than one leader's eyes.

Remember that and this…

If you build the ministry, they *might* come.
If you build it, show it to them, ask them to help lead, and give them a place to serve, they will come!

TRAUMA CIRCLES:
I failed at seeing the real needs of those I served.

Lesson 4:

Eradicate trauma legacies.

Lesson 4:

Eradicate trauma legacies.

I have the awesome privilege of facilitating children's ministry workshops for pastors, Christian education leaders, and children's ministry workers from across this nation. Some come looking for activity suggestions. Others want strategies to build a vibrant ministry composed of pomp and circumstance. They never get those exact answers from me.

Though I have knowledge of a few pomp-like circumstances and fun activities, I do not offer those upfront. Nor do I spend too much time talking about either. There are two reasons for that. One-I know little about their ministry contexts which makes me ill-equipped to oversee the construction of their ministries. Two- I don't want to…even if I had the best activity plans inclusive of the most attractive kid ventures.

I don't want to because I know those things would fall short of creating a need-meeting ministry. If I prescribed the same activities and routines for every ministry, most would fail. One size does not fit all. The variations among the churches—sizes, leadership teams, budgets, etc.—guarantee that the prescription would be too narrow for some and too loose for others. Furthermore, attraction-based ministry doesn't fit anyone.

Pardon my bluntness but this must be said. Attraction-based ministry presents the church as only being good for fun. And when the activities are no longer fun, children lose interest in coming to church. When the activities can no longer turn their attention away from the trials and tribulations they face daily, they lose hope in the church. The church becomes a mute idol, powerless to help. Powerless to heal.

In chapter one I asked you to identify your audience. That goes far beyond deciding on a targeted demographic. Identifying your audience includes knowing what the children and families in your sphere are going through, have been through, and could potentially face in the future. It sounds like a lot to do, but I am not talking about running a background check on potential attendees. This requires a simple inventory of what has unfolded in recent history. Look at the news, local and global. Examine what has happened or is happening that might leave a trauma legacy. Those things, whatever the findings, must guide the activities, services, and overall purpose of the ministry.

Activities are fun. Useful. Necessary. But the priority is to present a Jesus who walks with us through trauma.

So, identify the traumas surrounding your target audience.

Ask:

What global trauma might have the parents of this age group experienced?

In 2009, scientists, knowing that trauma to a pregnant woman affected at least three generations, began questioning whether trauma before pregnancy could do the same. They conducted experiments on a group of rats and found, "A mother who experienced trauma prior to becoming pregnant affects the emotional and social behavior of her offspring.[1]" Scientists suggest, since we too are mammals with

---

[1] University of Haifa. "Trauma Experienced By A Mother Even Before Pregnancy Will Influence Her Offspring's Behavior." ScienceDaily. ScienceDaily, 13 May 2009.
<www.sciencedaily.com/releases/2009/05/090512093301.htm>.

some of the same functionality, those findings are also true for mankind.

Current day example- 9/11 occurred twenty years ago. We are ministering to children whose parents experienced a nation-wide terror. It is very possible that some of the mal social and emotional behaviors exhibited in today's youth can be attributed to that specific historical trauma.

> "A mother who experienced trauma prior to becoming pregnant affects the emotional and social behavior of her offspring.[1]"

The COVID-19 pandemic will have that same effect. Twenty years from now, children who did not directly experience it will feel its wrath. Jim Cress, a licensed therapist, in an episode of Theology and Therapy[2] had this to say about trauma, "If it's hysterical. It's historical." Meaning traumas encountered long ago often present in frantic or frenzied present-day behaviors.

---

[2] Jim Cress, MA, LPC, CSAT, CMAT, "Therapy and Theology: The signs, symptoms, and cures of emotional immaturity. April 6, 2021

How does that apply to the way we plan to serve children? It helps us to understand a principle Jesus practiced: regulation before reach. We see that in Mark 5:1-20 and Luke 8:26-38. The story of a demon possessed man. Let's call him D.P. Man.

D.P. ran around naked, cutting himself, screaming and yelling, night and day in the town's graveyard. Jesus doesn't tell D.P. that He was the son of God, coming to save his soul. No. Jesus addressed what ailed D.P.- trauma. He regulated him before He did anything else because Jesus knew D.P. could never be reached if the things within were not dealt with.

Children and families immersed in trauma cannot be persuaded with cognitive, emotional, or spiritual arguments. The "demons" in their lives cannot be coaxed out with fun activities. They must first feel safe, regulated emotionally and physically, before they can open themselves to the gospel presentation. No pomp or circumstance can do that.

If you are crafting your ministry plan as you read—and I hope you are—write this down.

1. Our ministry must be a haven to the people it serves.
2. Ministry volunteers need trauma informed training.

Review your ministry set up. Does it consist of

offerings that can combat historical traumas?
i.e., Quiet spaces/routines for children who may be upset by the smallest of redirections. Individuals who can properly handle emotional breakdowns.

Ask:
Has the neighborhood experienced an economic downturn?

Trauma has more than one breeding ground. We tend to only think of it as synonymous with violence. It also grows itself in the desert of need. Scarcity creates a desperateness that can push individuals into behaviors that look self-centered or greedy, but really are survival techniques. Someone who has never had enough will fight to get what they need. Well adapted adults mistake those behaviors as savage and cannot understand why anyone would act that way, especially a child.

You're still writing that plan, right?
Grab your pen and add this third, oh so important, thing.

3. The best constructed children's ministries offer services beyond Sunday morning. Services that relieve needs and clears the mind to see and accept Jesus' salvation invitation.
   i.e. Feeding programs, clothing closets, or after school care. Things that help families survive

financial crises. Necessary services to keep children from resorting to survival mode tactics that may make a bad situation worse.

This bears repeating. Effective children's ministry reaches out to regulate the way Jesus did. Jesus, always, always, met physical needs before speaking to spiritual needs. Why? Because He understood how closely connected all those things are. Unfortunately, we don't. Well, I will not speak for you. I didn't. During my children's minister days, I was a Jesus pusher. Not in a good way. My best efforts were thwarted by believing the gospel and its power were housed in words instead of actions. Many days I tried to regulate the children and workers with a *what would Jesus do* attitude. That never works. It only creates church hurt, not healing. Don't make the same mistake.

Ask:

What personal traumas might the targeted demographic have experienced?

Getting to this question's answer without asking uncomfortable personal questions might seem impossible. Not so. There are two ways to get this information.

One- include this question on the ministry enrollment form: Is there anything you want to share about your child that will help us to adjust to his style of learning, communicating, and socializing? This question is a straightforward way of letting parents know that the ministry is interested in serving their child well. It also opens the door for parents to willingly share information.

They may not divulge deep family secrets, but most will give enough insight for the ministry workers to begin developing a relationship with the child.

Two- be vigilant. Look for behaviors that may point to problems at home, school, or with learning. Trauma informed training will help.

Ask:

Does our ministry plan encourage ministering up or down?

I have struggled with an appropriate way to explain this. Each explanation thus far felt offensive. My goal is to open awareness…not to offend.

Ministering up requires knowing that the children and families you serve are not lower-level humans. God did not make any of us less than. Always treat those being served with dignity regardless of their circumstances. A great rule of thumb- treat everyone with the love and respect that we say the pastor deserves but leave out the ridicule and unrealistic expectations he often gets. I wish you could see me bowled over with laughter. I crack myself up. Though my statement is funny, it is not a joke. Minister—don't pity.

Here's the final question.
Why does any of this matter?

How can the way a ministry operates eradicate trauma legacies?

Traumatized children and families lived steeped in their circumstances. Most likely the negativity runs through their minds day and night. Constantly dwelling on the negative ultimately stunts brain development. Negative thinking coupled with stunted brain development equals hopelessness.

Dr. Caroline Leaf, neuroscientist and author of *The Perfect You*, describes the brain and mind as being separate. The mind controls the brain. It determines how well the brain does what it was designed to do.

"Not only do we direct our behavioral, emotional, and intellectual changes, we also create structural change in our brains and bodies as a result of our individualistic and complex thinking processes.[3]" (The Perfect You, 26)

---

[3] Leaf, Caroline. *The Perfect You.* 2017 Baker Books. Grand Rapids,

That means that the brain can grow and thrive if the mind is filled with hope. We, the church, are the vehicles to that hope. If we intentionally target the negatives affecting those in our ministry spheres, we exchange their negatives for positives. Those positives now run through their minds which signal the brain to change from hopelessness to hope. Hope filled people change their worlds and those around them.

It matters.

It matters whether the ministry God has entrusted to you meets needs or provides attractive activities. The right choice will change present day circumstances and reach far into the future.

TEACHING TRUTH:
I almost failed at curriculum selection.

Lesson 5:

Everything should have a teaching component and all teaching components should teach truth.

Lesson 5:

Everything should have a teaching component and all teaching components should teach truth.

"I want to gather a group of writers and produce the next Vacation Bible School (VBS) curriculum," these words blindsided my pastor husband over a Saturday night dinner. He squinted a look I can't quite describe, and replied, "No."

Bowled over I countered, "Why not?" This after I had spent an entire Saturday afternoon mapping out themes for the children's ministry Wednesday night studies: focal and memory scriptures, talking points, corresponding activities, and prop suggestions. The only things missing were music and snack suggestions. I was pretty proud of my efforts and felt amped and able to take it to the next level. I repeated myself because obviously he didn't understand what I asked.

"No."

Again, without explanation.

I learned a lesson that day. The pastor does not have to explain his answer to the children's minister even if she is his wife. You can't see it, but there is an imaginary sad face emoji here.

Years later and with a few failures to win under my belt, I understand. My pastor husband knew a simple Saturday of lesson planning does not a curriculum writer make.

So, let's talk about all things curriculum using the lesson I learned as our guide.

Concerning curriculum ask:

1. What does it teach about God?

Just because it is produced by a Christian publisher does not mean it contains truths about God. Be sure that first and foremost, God is presented as supreme, three-in-one, and holy. Check to make sure Jesus is presented as a part of the Trinity and as maker, ruler, sustainer, and savior of the world. And The Holy Spirit also as a part of the Trinity, comforter, and as the one who lives within mankind's heart. If these truths are absent, it has no value.

Ask:

2. Does the curriculum teach me/the teacher?

A good curriculum includes teaching guides. Had I written VBS material that year, I would not have considered all the teaching components. In my Saturday efforts, I included one teaching suggestion for each lesson omitting differentiation for age, ability, group size, and special needs.

I feel like one of those stick figures that is often included on social media memes recalling some blunderous mishap should accompany each of these questions captioned: This is Brenda. Brenda didn't consider these things. Don't be like Brenda.

Ask:
3. Will this curriculum teach the children we serve?

Think about the children and the experiences they might have had. Are the examples within the curriculum relevant? Are the wording and style applicable to their lives?

Ask:
4. Can the children we serve mentally digest the theological objectives?

The curriculum you choose should show a clear pattern of development introducing truths about God that build with anticipated cognitive growth. First graders will not understand a lesson about the

Godhead. Some adults still struggle with this idea. Appropriate children's ministry curriculum will present foundational concepts that lead to greater understanding later.

Ask:
5. Are the activities correlated with the lesson?

If the curriculum meets every other standard but this one, this is not a deal breaker. But you should know, meaningful movement increases retention. Activities that reinforce lessons help the learner to understand the concept. And…here's the kicker. When that activity is performed in a different context under different circumstances, the lesson's concepts will resurface. How awesome is that?

Correlating lesson activities are not a must have.

Know Your Curriculum!

The curriculum you choose should show a clear pattern of development introducing truths about God that build with anticipated cognitive growth.

They are, however, wonderful teaching tools that follow the learner wherever they go.

Ask:

6. Are the lesson and teaching guides diverse?

Diverse in age- Do some of the teaching examples or stories place emphasis on the importance of the elderly?

Diverse in ability- Are there representations of children who learn, move, or communicate differently?

Diverse in culture- Don't just think about skin color here. My African American experience growing up in southeastern Virginia is vastly different from my cousins' who grew up in Northern Virginia. Same bloodline, same state, two different experiences. Therefore, think- various ways of doing things in the four quadrants: north, south, east, and west. Think- various ways families communicate. Think- various environments.

Ask:

7. Is the curriculum easily modifiable and accessible?

Spoiler alert: no curriculum is perfect. Most will need a little modification. The goal is modification, not complete reconstruction. If the material looks completely different after modification, try another curriculum.

Some examples of slight modifications:

- Exchanging songs for cultural context or to reinforce the lesson
- Revamping one or two examples to coincide with the environment or current local or world news
- Switching activities or props to accommodate for lack of space or resources

One note of caution- do not choose a curriculum solely based on cultural appropriateness. Choose material that displays a true representation of God.

Finally—and this is not a deal breaker either—not yet. We live in the digital age. Digital access is a welcome bonus. There are several benefits, two important ones come to mind. Digital access allows us to legally share with a bigger audience. I won't tell all the horror stories of churches making copies of copyrighted work. Digital access removes this temptation. Last, but so helpful—digital access ultimately saves money and natural resources. No explanation needed.

One last discussion before concluding this chapter and heading toward the two mini chapters that will end our time together.

Ask:
8. Should we write and produce our own Bible study curriculum?

Seeing how this chapter opened, you might guess my answer is no. Surprise! It's not. Why? I firmly believe God's word. 1 Corinthians 12 gives an overview of the body of Christ. In that body are many parts, equipped with many gifts. The underlying message is that every gift known to mankind is contained within the universal Body of Christ. Because that is true, I believe every branch of the body, local churches—yours and mine, have within its walls every gift it needs to accomplish the work God designed it to accomplish.

Understand what I am implying. Your church does not have every gift known to mankind within its walls. Neither does mine. We do, however, have every gift needed to minister to the people within and without our walls.

So, should you write Bible study curriculum? Yes, if that is what God is calling your team to do. That will be evident by Him providing men and women gifted to produce with a spirit of excellence and intentionality. I didn't have that during my time as a children's minister. Do you?

Write Bible study curriculum if:

- There is a resident theologian within your reach- someone who has a thorough understanding of systematic theology. If that someone has never heard of systematic theology. They are not the one—look for another.
- There is someone within your reach who can accurately exegete scripture. Again, if the person you have in mind must reach for the dictionary to know whether exegeting is in their wheelhouse—they are not the one, look for another.
- There is an individual who can take the theologian's work coupled with the exegete's work and draw parallels between Middle Eastern biblical history, current and future events, and can produce age-appropriate children's lessons. If said individual does not know Jewish boys were required to memorize the first five books of the Bible by age ten or so—look for another.
- There is a thoughtful individual who can take the produced lessons and implement a variety of teaching and learning methods with considerations for learning disabilities. There's a chance your ministry may be able to write

Bible study curriculum. But don't get excited yet.

- There is a spatially astute, energetic challenge seeker who can and will glean from the other four disciplines and create activities that are doable in the children's ministry space and reinforces the lesson objectives.

If within your local church, you have all these individuals, you are halfway there. Missing from that list is: music director, content editor, grammar editor, line editor, and some more folks I can't think of right now.

Should you write Bible study curriculum? Yes, only if you understand it will take more than one Saturday afternoon and must involve knowledgeable individuals trained in the necessary areas.

MINISTRY POSSIBILITIES-COULDS NOT SHOULDS:
I failed to differentiate between ministry must haves and ministry wants.

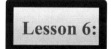

Don't try to do everything but do something.

> Sunday morning Bible studies should include a bible lesson of course, but also—worship: song(s) and scripture, scripture memorization, and an activity or craft.

Lesson 6:

Don't try to do everything but do something.

Spiritual Disciplines in Worship

In chapter four, I intentionally tried to steer everyone away from centering ministry plans around activities. But I also expressed the necessity of them too. Let's make a deal. I will list some ministry suggestions and the reasons behind them if you promise not to duplicate them. Instead, use my suggestions as a springboard to craft activities and events that meet the demands and culture of your environment.

I'll start with this tidbit: midweek and/or Sunday morning Bible studies should include a bible lesson of course, but also—worship: song(s) and scripture, scripture memorization, and an activity or craft. Why?

This practice introduces spiritual disciplines.

Can I confess something? I first heard this term in my early thirties. I'd been in church all my life without it so much as passing by my ear gates. Not kidding. My mother accepted Jesus as savior on our living room sofa while one year old me held onto her knee. Yet, I had never heard the term spiritual disciplines. The good news—my mother practiced them daily. Which helped me to settle into spiritual disciplines as a lifestyle.

My point? Practicing these things as a life necessity and with intentionality lays a foundation of understanding. Children will see the disciplines as a part of a relationship with God—how to get to know Him—even if they cannot identify the practices with a technical term. Not knowing the term may have been better for me. I began practicing those things because I saw how the interactions connected my mother to God, and the way her time with Him steadied her during crisis. I wanted that, not a ritual. That is what we want for the children in our ministries.

Activities Too

It is easy to see why spiritual disciplines are important, but what about activities? Why are they a necessary part of worship? We have briefly mentioned one reason: if properly planned, an activity is a great reinforcement tool. There is another principle at work too. It can be a refocusing tool as well. Kids have short attention spans, ever increasingly so because of electronic games, digitally enhanced movies, and such. After sitting for a fifteen-minute Bible lesson, an activity gives their brains a stretch break, an opportunity to refocus. Bible study activities fit that bill. Lastly, activities give children an outlet to do what their young bodies and brains must do—move.

Children learn through touch and by interacting with their environment. Please let them move.

Bible Study Activities

Let's continue by acknowledging that Bible study activities and ministry activities are different. The first is an activity carried out during Sunday morning or mid-week Bible study. It can be used to reinforce a current lesson, as a connecting bridge between two lessons, or to introduce the theme for the next lesson.

The following charts contain sample lessons and corresponding activities. Review the examples. Take note of the ideas and concepts. Tweak them to fit your ministry context and curriculum. Also note, the lessons examples are not fully fleshed out, as they are examples and not intended for use as is.

Focus on the Bible study activities. Can any be used in your context? Draw applicable ideas and concepts from them for your ministry setting.

God's Power on Display- David and Goliath, The Series		
Bible Lesson	Bible Study Activity	Purpose/Use
Goliath the Big 1 Samuel 17:1-10	Compose a rap song for each set of verses. Create a Tik Tok video of the children performing the rap. Be sure to use an account specifically dedicated to the church's children's ministry. *Obtain parental permission. Create an alternative for children whose parents wish to opt out of social media use.	Verse by verse scripture memorization techniques Encourages students to want to learn an entire chapter of the bible. Examples an interesting way to engage with and learn scripture. Also, creating the rap will help the students think about how the scripture applies to their context.
No One to Fight 1 Samuel 17:11-16		
An Interested Party 1 Samuel 17:17-27		
An Unlikely Volunteer 1 Samuel 17:28-37		
Suited for Battle 1 Samuel 17:38-45		
A Fight to Remember 1 Samuel 17:46-50		

*Lesson and correlating activities are an example of a teaching series inclusive of a long-term/on-going project.

Bible Lesson	Bible Study Activity	Materials Needed	Instructions	Purpose/Use
God Sees Us: Gideon in the Winepress	**Where's Waldo:** Scripture Edition	Magnifying glasses, scripture passages in small print on large chart paper (collage style)	Pair students. Allow 5-10 Minutes for each team to search for predetermined scriptures related to the lesson. The pair finding the most scriptures are the winners.	Reinforces or introduces a lesson. Could use to make the point- God's sight is greater than a magnifying glass. We can't always see what we are looking for, but He always finds us.

Ministry Activities

The second type of activity will typically take the children on an adventure and/or give them an opportunity to hone or discover a skill or gift

When planning a ministry activity ask two questions: How will this glorify God? In what ways will the children be strengthened/built up?

First a few tips:

- Develop annual ministry activities/events, others occurring every other year or so.

For example, Summer Day Camp as an annual event. It gives parents a reliable childcare option. A weekend retreat for 5th and 6th graders every two years. It could serve as a rite of passage, something for the younger students to look forward to.
- Have at least two intergenerational ministry activities per year. Make the event inviting enough for ages 2-92. This helps to bridge the relational gap between the age groups. Intergenerational activities liven the lives of the older generation and enriches and empowers the younger generation.
- Construct a general emergency plan for events/activities, as needed. Have ministry leaders/workers review it thoroughly before each event. Tweak according to the activity/event.

See the following chart for ministry activities suggestions.

Ministry Activity/Service	Children are Edified/Built Up
Oratorical Contest	Public speaking practice
Writing Circle	Encouraging written expression
Sporting Event Outing	Bonding and fun
Children's Retreat: 5th and 6th grade	New experiences, Rite of passage
Young Investors	Increase financial awareness
Computer Coding Ministry	Preparing for the future
Clothes Closet	Meeting needs of current membership and the surrounding neighbors
Early African Church History courses for the older children	Implement as a rite of passage. Helps children (of all ethnicities) to establish a concrete understanding of the origins of Christianity and refute the idea of Christianity being "the white man's religion," forced upon African slaves.

Choose activities according to the needs within your ministry. Children from lower socio-economic backgrounds might benefit more from an event outing as their parents' budget does not allow for such extracurriculars. Or a child immersed in a less diverse environment may benefit from the Early African Church History courses. As relationships develop between ministry workers and those being served, choosing appropriate ministry activities becomes clearer.

So, I will close this section with a challenge: Spend three to six months getting to know the children you serve. Play word association games to help you see how they think. Have a storytelling hour. Divide children into circles of five. Present pictures from magazines and have them take turns creating stories from the pictures. This will give great insight into their worldview and direct you in choosing ministry activities that will help them see God in every aspect of life.

Friends, I know this is not an easy task. I am praying for you, and I believe you can do it. Don't focus on numbers, accolades, or accomplishments. Focus on God and where He is leading the ministry. You will not fail to win in your service efforts. That I can promise.

QUIT EVERY DAY AND TWO TIMES ON SUNDAY:
I almost failed at making room for quit.

Lesson 7:

Sabbath rest is not a suggestion; it is a must.

"When work is an idol, rest will feel like a sin."-

Josh Teis

Lesson 7:

Sabbath rest is not a suggestion; it is a must.

I briefly mentioned Sabbath in one of the opening chapters. Don't equate its importance with those fleeting remarks or the order in which it occurs in the chapter lineup. Remember the Sabbath and keep it holy for children's ministry leaders and workers is the straw that will break the camel's back if not observed. Remember, as in make it a priority not a passing thought. Remember as in, reserving this discussion for last, is an intentional placement in your mind's final thoughts category with the goal of it resting at the heart or your ministry.

SABBATH – Confession and Advice

Some say confession is good for the soul and not for the character. I don't agree. Confession frees the soul and polishes the character. Let me do a little soul clearing and character shining with this confession: I did not consider Sabbath as something to do until recently. As a matter of fact, during my tenure as a children's minister, I didn't consider it at all. Major mistake for me. A blessing for you. My fumble emboldened this advice, "Quit children's ministry every day." And I say that without one ounce of trepidation. I am as serious about this as Southerners are about their sweet tea. You know that's serious.

Quit every day…doubly so for full-time staff members. Quit every day, two times on Sunday, and at least once a year. I really want to say four times a year, but you might stop reading and count me as insane before I tell you why quitting is necessary.

QUIT EVERY DAY

God quit every day during the creation process.

Read Genesis 1 later. Pay special attention to verses five, eight, thirteen, nineteen, twenty-three, and thirty-one. I'll tell you now what each verse reveals- a cessation of the creation work from evening until morning. A complicated way of saying God quit working every day and began each new day from a place of rest. On most of those creation days, He also looked at what He created before moving on to the next thing. Of course, Almighty God did not need literal rest, but He stopped working. There must be a reason why. Here's what I believe:

-Rest for humanity's sake: God knew mankind needed physical rest. He also knew we needed an example. In His divine wisdom, He created rest on the first day of creation, modeled it, and later mandated it.

-Rest to Observe: On just about every creation day, God stopped working and looked at His work. *He saw* His creation. That phrase, "He saw" could be translated as appreciated. For us, resting to observe is an opportunity to appreciate God's work within our ministry efforts. Observational rest—slowing down and looking at the work from a place of stillness helps us to see our efforts for what they are—human, and God's efforts for what they are—supernatural. This type of rest puts the burden of success where it belongs, on God rather than on us.

-Rest so that the created things could fulfill their individual and collective purposes: When God stopped working on creation, creation started working for Him. Purpose awakened in each thing He created. For example, God created light, observed it as good, and then rested. Light, from that moment until this one, arrives daily. Same with night. God rested from creating night, but it, too, makes its debut at the close of every day. The two work hand in hand, yet from their individual purposes, establishing what we know as a full day. Our ministries should reflect a similar individual and collective reproductive power. When we rest, the purpose in our ministry awakens and unceasingly does what it was created to do and connects with what God has already established.

Effective ministry happens when we do what we can and trust God with the rest. Rest as in remaining tasks and rest as in cessation of work. Translation- What we *can do* should not consume 12-14 hours of the day, seven days a week. There must be a designated stopping point each day.

At Your Best author, Carey Nieuwhof, suggests all human beings have a best clock [my words not his], three to five hours of peak cognitive ability. Study your body rhythm to determine where your best hours fall on the clock. Dedicate that time to the most important tasks (cognitively challenging ones). Keeping in mind that what goes up must come down. Our best clocks have a median and low work range. Tasks that take little to no brain power should be scheduled on the low end and everything else in between.

Create a task schedule that coincides with your most efficient work times and stick to it. When the tasks are done, and even when they aren't, but you have given your best effort, quit. Raise your hand and repeat after me. "I will assign the tasks appropriately, tackle them accordingly, and release them at the end of the day." Make this your solemn pledge. Trust God's faithfulness and rest while He does the work. We take our roles too seriously sometimes. If you are actively following the vision and plans God laid out, and something goes wrong or unfinished, you should not work beyond exhaustion to make it right. I know…this goes against everything your mama taught you. Hard work is honorable, but hard work without trust in God is just hard and it doesn't work.

Quit Two Times on Sunday

Reread the previous section. Welcome its principles into your heart and mind as you read this one. You are going to need them.

There are two types of quitting needed on Sundays. The first is what you read previously. I know what you're thinking. *Sunday is a workday. I can't quit on Sunday.* It is, but it has an end, doesn't it? God's prescribed Sabbath says rest is preceded by six days of work. When the sun sets on Sunday, quit.

While at church note the things that went well, awry, and/or questionable. Leave those notes in your office, car, or somewhere out of reach, and rest. Whatever situation—except for extreme emergencies like negligence or death, God forbid, leave them alone for the next twenty-four hours. Nothing you do will rewind the clock and change missteps, or even make celebratory moments greater. Take the day off. Or, let me say it like Grandma would say it, "Sit down somewhere and rest."

The second quit requires mental and emotional discipline. Quit or rest from straying away from your designated role. If you are the ministry leader, lead the ministerial musts. If you are a cleaner, step into that role and stay there. Teacher, teach. Coordinators, corral your assigned age group.

I know what you are thinking again. *Brenda Michelle, that makes absolutely no sense. If I do that, something will be lacking.* Great, you read my mind too. Let the missing elements surface. Resting from picking up the slack reveals the areas of lack. Many of us are so accustomed to just doing what needs to be done—and complaining about it along the way—that no one else can see the deficits. Unseen things get no attention. So rest, quit filling in all the roles and do what you are assigned. This is why so many workers are worn out and frustrated with ministry.

You're thinking again, aren't you?

Well, what am I supposed to do?

If the areas of deficit might cause harm or leave the children susceptible to danger, of course meet that need immediately. For others, begin working on the recruitment plan again (Operation Covered), after assessing what new positions/roles/volunteers are needed. You may have to go as far as limiting the number of children you can serve. Better that, than risking a situation that will put you, the church, its leadership, and the goal of the ministry in jeopardy.

Quit Once a Year

Take a vacation. No explanation needed. Right? Staycation, toes in sandcation, doesn't matter. Just vacate the church premises physically and mentally.

That's a no-brainer, but here's what might not

be so obvious. The ministry needs a vacation at least twice a year. One vacation for ministry workers to rejuvenate and another for the ministry to do the same. What do I mean? It's not uncommon for churches to do a church wide ministry break during the Summer. Quite a few use this time for ministry planning and regrouping. Well, that ain't no vacation for the workers. Yes, I said ain't. I hope you felt its impact. As out of place and tacky as ain't is here, so are ministry workers who lack a proper break.

I think it wise to use the Summer break as a ministry rejuvenation. Look at the wins, strengths, and failures from the first six or seven months, revamp what needs revamping, and add, subtract, or rearrange workers, activities, etc. as necessary. This is also a time of planning activities or implementing new ideas for the upcoming year. Boom! Ministry rejuvenation.

Designate the last three weeks of the year for ministry workers to take a break from serving the children and planning. No worries about being ready for the new year because that planning took place during the ministry rejuvenation vacation. Genius, I know…except your brain is running faster than a race between Usain Bolt and Sha'Carri Richardson. Let me see if I can snatch one of those thoughts rounding the curves of your dendrites. You are thinking: *Well, that sounds ideal, but the problem is, it's ideal. It will not work in real life.*

Aww Friend. Think positive and plan according to your ministry environment. No ministry is alike and as genius as my suggestions are, some tweaking is necessary. But if you decide that none will work in your context, it won't. Not because it's idyllic, but because you relegated it as such without even trying to bring it into the realistic realm.

One More Quick Quit Note
Earlier under the Confession and Advice section I intimated that quitting four times during the year was necessary but refrained from going any further for fear of you thinking I'd taken this sabbath thing too far. Now, I can unburden my soul and gloss my character again by confessing that I already introduced the concept. Either you missed it or forgot altogether. Sabbath is embedded in the Build Your Team chapter. Operation Covered, done correctly, ensures small sabbath times for ministry workers throughout the year.

The intent was not to deceive you.

I promise.

Rest is so important that I slipped the idea of it in one form or another throughout the book.

For your good and God's glory.

The ultimate sabbath as it pertains to our topic is resting from the idea that success is built on win upon win. When in fact, the opposite is true. Success' foundation and four walls are held up and knit together by our failures. Failing and retrying in children's ministry is the only way to produce solid wins for the kingdom. So, if you are failing just know that you are on the road to a win.

BESTING BEHAVIORS:
I failed at behavior management.

Bonus

Get the ministry attendees on the right bus, AND in the right seat.

Bonus

Get the ministry attendees on the right bus, AND in the right seat.

Though *Failing to Win* is a short book, it presents a lot to digest and wrestle through. Which is why it needed to be short and to the point. But I couldn't end without a little advice on how to manage behavior.

Two words: routine and ability. Implementing and accessing these two will squash most behavior issues. Trust me on this.

Routines

Take time and establish a routine for everything the ministry does: big and small.

- Restroom breaks
- Entering and leaving learning spaces
- Snack

- Play Centers
- Parent pick-up
- Asking and answering questions
- EVERYTHING

Routines alert everyone to the expectations of the environment. I learned this as a preschool teacher. Using a routine, I taught three-year-old students to stand up, quietly push their chairs under, and line up without talking. In addition, after the first two weeks of school, I never returned one toy to its place, collected papers, or put reading books back on shelves. The three-year-olds did it all. How? We practiced. I spent the first two weeks of the year developing and modeling class routines. When new students arrived later in the year, the other students acclimated them to the inner workings of our world.

Two main ingredients in behavior disasters are no routine or loosely followed routines. If students and teachers alike do not know what to do, they do what they want to do. This, friend, will result in unwanted behaviors all around. Create and strictly follow routines.

One last note on routines—they do not equate to boredom or take away fresh expressions. A properly placed routine should move everyone from one activity to the next without lull. Everything in between can, and should be, filled with age-appropriate excitement.

Review the 2nd and 3rd graders sample routine and activities chart. Note how the routines stay the same but the learning activities change.

Routine	Instructions	Activity
Beginning Bible Study/Sunday School	Start soft music before students arrive. Have students sit in pre-assigned spots on the carpet. (Criss-cross Applesauce-legs folded in front of them.) Children are instructed to pick up awaiting bibles and begin quietly "reading" the scripture lesson for the day. (Yes, they will talk to one another, and no they probably won't read. What they will be is all seated and accounted for, not wild and crazy...running around the room.) The music swells a bit to get their attention, then is turned off. Students are instructed to put bibles down and turn attention to teacher for their next directive.	**1st Sunday:** Bible lesson taught through mime. **2nd Sunday:** Bible lesson taught using tangible objects to make lesson come alive. **3rd Sunday:** Bible lesson read in popcorn style reading. Teacher uses guided questions to help students articulate the lesson's meaning. **4th Sunday:** Bible lesson is taught through storytelling. Students are given five minutes to compose one question each. The teacher will select students one at a time to pose their questions to the group.

*Routines and activities are examples.

Routine	Instructions	Activity
Transitioning from Bible Study to Arts and Crafts	Soft music starts again signaling the students to return bibles and themselves back to their starting positions (Carpet-Criss-cross Applesauce). There they await arts and crafts instructions. Once instructions are given, students quietly move to the arts and crafts area, one at a time, according to their positioning on the carpet. Teacher stops music signifying that each student is in place and craft time can begin.	**1st Sunday:** Create a no-bake sweet-treat recipe that coincides with the lesson. **2nd Sunday:** Recreate bible lesson through pictures using a round-robin style. Give each student a different color marker. Assign each a small part of the bible lesson to draw. While one illustrates the others are assisting with verbal clues. This will get noisy. The goal is for students to have exciting exchanges throughout the process. **3rd Sunday:** Present three craft options related to the bible lesson. Allow students to choose which one they want to create. **4th Sunday:** Have students chose one character from the bible lesson. Provide clay and small Styrofoam heads for students to sculpt their chosen character. This kind of activity is best suited for a series lesson as it may take a few Sundays to complete.

Create routines and activities that fit the culture, curriculum, and budget of your ministry. Will some of the precious littles act out even while following solid, consistent routines? Yes. The good news is that you will have a routine in place, something concrete to redirect them toward the desired behavior.

No routine

Teacher- "Harper, stop yelling and sit down right now!"

Harper- *blank stare* More yelling and running around.

Routine

Teacher- "Harper, what are we supposed to be doing right now?"

Harper- *looks around* "It's quiet reading time." *More running around and yelling

Teacher- "Are you reading quietly?

Harper- "No."

Teacher- "Please join the rest of us on the carpet in your assigned spot and start reading quietly."

Harper- *reluctantly returns to the carpet. *

Okay, so that is a best-case scenario. I know it won't go as smoothly in real life. What will happen is Harper will have clear directives, knows what's expected, and the teacher doesn't escalate the situation making the environment a hostile one for Harper.

This is my lived experience. It takes a few tries to get a Harper-like child routine acclimated. When it happens, it happens.

Ability

"Every student on the right bus...AND, in the right seat."

It was the AND that caught my attention as I sat in a summer retreat session taught by our new school principal. These words were her secret sauce to student success. Not sure if they originated with her, but I am sure the sauce works. Therefore, I am passing them on to you as the second tool in behavior management.

Her phrase can be understood in its expanded form to mean: *Make sure learners are learning the right things, at the right time, and with personalized instruction;* and, can be whittled down to: *Teach according to learning style and understanding.*

I understood what she meant by every student on the right bus as it pertained to student success.

But she shocked me with the second portion of the statement. I realized I'd never considered that being in the right learning environment with the right teaching tools was still not enough to ensure success. I was the office manager at the time with no formal teaching training. So, my lack of consideration is understandable. This may be true of you too. Maybe you have not considered what might be obvious to teaching professionals in the former principal's words.

You want to manage behavior issues? Challenge advanced thinkers and raise the thinking of a cognitively challenged child. Both require scaffolding of some sort. Both leave little room for misbehaving.

> *Make sure learners are learning the right things, at the right time, and with personalized instruction…*
>
> J. Harrison-Coleman

All "bad" behaviors have a root. In case you missed it in the earlier discussion, one of those roots is the lack of a plan/routine/direction. Another is failing to correctly assess a child's ability. Children get distracted when learning materials either go over or fall beneath their level of understanding.

Think of it this way. A student who can process information beyond their chronological age and estimated ability functions best when guided into a deeper understanding of new information. They long for it, even if they don't know that's what they long for. In a slow-moving teaching/learning environment, they need something to feed their intellect. That is when behaviors start to go awry. For most, the intent is not to get into trouble. They simply are seeking more learning opportunities. Conversely, the student who does not understand…wants to understand but may not have the words to express that. Frustration ensues. Trouble erupts. He too only wants to feed his intellect. Our job is to identify how our learners learn and teach accordingly.

How do we do that? Relationship.

An amendment to my two-word solution to behavior management is needed. Want to manage behaviors? Three words, routine, ability, and relationship. That is what my principal meant in a nutshell. Establish routines that give space to grow relationships. Growing relationships then give space to assess what the children can and can't do. All of this takes time. Well spent time.

This bonus section is especially important and useful if the children's ministry is full of children who are being raised in a home environment worlds apart from how the children's ministry team members were raised. Without implementing behavior management, the ministry could evolve into administering something other than God's lovingkindness and grace-laced discipline. Determine that the ministry will be a place where children will not be yelled at, belittled, or ostracized because of "bad" behavior. Grow a routine-oriented team. The end-result for all involved will be well worth the sacrifice.

Don't worry! If God called you to this ministry, you can do it. Take everything you have read within these pages to God in prayer. Seek Him for direction. There is no way you can fail to win.

Love to you all,

Brenda

Endnotes

University of Haifa. "Trauma Experienced By A Mother Even Before Pregnancy Will Influence Her Offspring's Behavior." ScienceDaily. 13 May 2009. <www.sciencedaily.com/releases/2009/05/090512093301.htm>

Cress, Jim. "Therapy and Theology: The signs, symptoms, and cures of emotional immaturity. April 6, 2021.

Leaf, Caroline. *The Perfect You.* 2017 Baker Books. Grand Rapids, MI.

Sketchy Sermons via Facebook 4/25/22.

Made in the USA
Columbia, SC
19 September 2023